W.E.B. DU BOIS

The African-American Biographies Series

—African-American Biographies—

W. E. B. DU BOIS

Champion of Civil Rights

Series Consultant:
Dr. Russell L. Adams, Chairman
Department of Afro-American Studies, Howard University

Mark Rowh

Enslow Publishers, Inc.

40 Industrial Road   PO Box 38
Box 398   Aldershot
Berkeley Heights, NJ 07922   Hants GU12 6BP
USA   UK

http://www.enslow.com

To the English faculty at West Virginia State College

Library of Congress Cataloging-in-Publication Data

Rowh, Mark.
    W. E. B. Du Bois : champion of civil rights / Mark Rowh.
      p. cm. — (African-American biographies)
    Includes bibliographical references and index.
    Summary: A biography of the noted historian and sociologist who was an important
leader of African American protest and helped found the National Association for the
Advancement of Colored People.
    ISBN 0-7660-1209-3
    1. Du Bois, W. E. B. (William Edward Burghardt), 1868–1963—Juvenile literature.
2. Afro-Americans—Biography—Juvenile literature. 3. National Association for the
Advancement of Colored People—Biography—Juvenile literature. 4. Civil rights
workers—United States—Biography—Juvenile literature. 5. Afro-American historians—
Biography—Juvenile literature. [1. Du Bois, W. E. B. (William Edward Burghardt),
1868–1963. 2. Civil rights workers. 3. Afro-Americans—Biography.] I. Title. II. Title:
WEB Du Bois. III. Title: William Edward Burghardt Du Bois. IV. Series.
E185.97.D73R69 1999
305.896′073′0092
[B]—DC21   98-50787
                                         CIP
                                         AC

Printed in the United States of America

10 9 8 7 6 5 4 3 2

To Our Readers: All Internet addresses in this book were active and appropriate
when we went to press. Any comments or suggestions can be sent by e-mail to
Comments@enslow.com or to the address on the back cover.

Every effort has been made to locate all copyright holders of material used in this book. If
any errors or omissions have occurred, corrections will be made in future editions of this
book.

Illustration Credits: Special Collections and Archives, W.E.B. Du Bois Library,
University of Massachusetts Amherst, pp. 13, 17, 21, 30, 37, 42, 53, 58, 67, 80, 91,
98, 103; Library of Congress, pp. 9, 62, 72; National Archives, Still Picture Branch,
pp. 51, 110; Photographs and Prints Division, Schomberg Center for Research in
Black Culture, The New York Public Library, Astor, Lenox and Tilden
Foundations, p. 25; Special Collections and University Archives, Rutgers
University Libraries, p. 88; University of Massachusetts Photographic Services,
p. 107.

Cover Illustration: Library of Congress

CONTENTS

Acknowledgments

The author would like to thank all those who made the development of this manuscript possible, including the following:

Dr. Sophia Nelson

Dr. Felix Paul

Dr. Melvin Anderson

Lisa and Jenny Rowh

The University of Massachusetts

The Library of Congress

The National Archives

West Virginia State College

1

VOICE OF
INSPIRATION

It was a hot day in August 1910 when a distinguished-looking gentleman reported for his first day on the job. He had traveled by train from Atlanta to New York City, eager to start work for a new organization known as the National Association for the Advancement of Colored People (NAACP).

The man was William E. B. Du Bois (pronounced *Du-Boyz*). He was already known for his outspoken demands for equal rights for his people. In 1909, Du Bois had helped found the NAACP. This group of activists, both black and white, was dedicated to justice and civil rights for all Americans. Now, in 1910, Du Bois had agreed to become the director of publications and research for the NAACP.

The United States at that time was a vastly different place from today. The concept of civil rights, or equal rights for all citizens, was not accepted. Segregation of the races was common practice. In fact, it was a matter of law. The United States Supreme Court, in a famous 1896 case known as *Plessy* v. *Ferguson*, had ruled that white Americans and black Americans were legally equal. It also ruled that it was legal to keep the two races separated. This meant that blacks and whites attended separate schools, lived apart from one another, and did almost everything else as if there were a boundary between them.

In reality, "separate" was not at all "equal." The opportunities for African Americans were very limited. Menial, low-paying jobs were the norm. African-American schools lacked funding. Especially in the South, African Americans were treated as second-class citizens in everything from voting to using public transportation. Too often, innocent blacks suffered mistreatment at the hands of whites. Sometimes this went to violent extremes, including beatings and lynchings. For African Americans at the beginning of the twentieth century, America was a very hostile place.

Du Bois wanted to change all this. He knew that before social conditions could improve, people all over

W. E. B. Du Bois

the United States needed to know more about the problems faced by African Americans. Information could lead to understanding—and to change. Du Bois saw the NAACP as an avenue for meeting this need. In those days, there was no radio and no television. The best way to reach large numbers of people was through newspapers, magazines, or speeches at public gatherings. Du Bois felt that in his new job, he could best fight for the rights of African Americans.[1]

From a career standpoint, taking a job with the new group was risky. His duties were vague, and financial support was uncertain. But Du Bois believed that the work of the NAACP was more important than his own welfare. He felt it was vital to let the country know that African Americans, known at the time as Negroes or colored people, were not being treated fairly. "I am willing to accept any reasonable risk," he had written in accepting the position, "for the privilege of engaging in a work which, I agree with you, is of paramount and critical importance."[2]

So Du Bois left his job as a professor at Atlanta University and moved to New York City. When he reported for work at NAACP headquarters, it was not even clear how Du Bois would be paid. "I don't know who is going to pay your salary. I have no money," said Oswald Villard, the group's director.[3] But Du Bois went ahead and got to work.

His first goal was to develop a new monthly

magazine. It would show both the good and the bad aspects of African-American life in the United States. Du Bois felt strongly that such a publication was greatly needed. Some leaders within the NAACP disagreed. They thought it would cost too much or fail to attract enough attention. But Du Bois persisted. Quickly he began the work needed to launch the magazine.

Du Bois's first few weeks with the NAACP were filled with activity. He asked several journalists to write articles for the new publication. He convinced them that this magazine could become the voice of the NAACP across the country. Their articles could provoke public discussion about the need for equal rights. Du Bois also wrote many of the articles himself. He saw his role not only as editor of the magazine, but as its main writer. He enjoyed writing and had a talent for turning out a large quantity of written material.

It was also Du Bois's job to publicize the magazine and arrange to have it printed. In September, Du Bois formally announced the publication and invited subscriptions. A year's subscription would cost "the nominal price of One Dollar."[4]

When it came time to name the magazine, Du Bois and others involved decided to call it *The Crisis*. They chose this name because they felt that the world was entering a critical time in history, especially in terms of human relations. This was not the first magazine of its type, but Du Bois hoped it would be the most outspoken and the best. It would also serve as the official publication of the NAACP.

In November 1910, the first issue of *The Crisis* was printed. It was sixteen pages long and sold for ten cents a copy. "The object of this publication is to set forth those facts and arguments which show the danger of race prejudice, particularly as manifested today toward colored people," Du Bois wrote in the premier issue.[5]

To that end, the magazine adopted a serious tone and focused on real-life instances of racial discrimination. One article reported a recent lynching—a black man had been hanged by a white mob. Another article covered the racially motivated shooting of an African-American man. Editorials dealt with issues such as segregated schools and other examples of discrimination. In one editorial, Du Bois wrote that some people might fear that *The Crisis* would cause too much "agitation," but "Agitation is a necessary evil to tell of the ills of the Suffering."[6]

The day *The Crisis* first appeared was an exciting one for Du Bois. He knew this was a major step forward. No other publication reported so extensively on African-American life. The new magazine promised to reveal problems of racial inequality. It would give readers the facts and opinions they needed to understand important racial issues.

THE CRISIS

A RECORD OF THE DARKER RACES

Volume One	MARCH, 1911	Number Five

Edited by W. E. BURGHARDT DU BOIS, with the co-operation of Oswald Garrison Villard, J. Max Barber, Charles Edward Russell, Kelly Miller, W. S. Braithwaite and M. D. Maclean.

.Egyptian Portrait of One of the Black Kings of the Upper Nile, Ra-Maat-Neb, Builder of Pyramid No. 17. (After Lepsius.)

PUBLISHED MONTHLY BY THE

National Association for the Advancement of Colored People

AT TWENTY VESEY STREET   NEW YORK CITY

ONE DOLLAR A YEAR   TEN CENTS A COPY

The Crisis, edited by Du Bois, reported on African-American life.

Du Bois was not disappointed. The first issue of *The Crisis* quickly sold out. It soon became obvious that more copies would be needed, and the number of copies printed was increased from 1,000 to 2,500 for the next issue.[7] *The Crisis* was on its way.

Development of *The Crisis* was a major accomplishment for Du Bois. It provided a vehicle for reaching thousands of Americans. Du Bois and other writers reported news of interest to African Americans and those who supported the cause of civil rights. More important, Du Bois had a platform to express his opinions on vital issues.

The long train ride from Atlanta, Georgia, had paid off. W. E. B. Du Bois had become the voice of the NAACP. At the same time, he emerged as an even more important leader for civil rights in America.

2

BRIGHT
YOUNGSTER

William Edward Burghardt Du Bois was born February 23, 1868, in Great Barrington, Massachusetts. He was an only child. His father was Alfred Du Bois, a native of Haiti who worked as a barber. His mother was Mary Silvina Burghardt Du Bois, a woman of African and Dutch ancestry.[1] Like most African Americans, Du Bois was descended from slaves. His great-great-grandfather had been a slave and was freed during the Revolutionary War.

At the time of William Du Bois's birth, the Civil War had been over less than three years. America was still recovering from the trauma of that great conflict, and the American South had entered a period of rebuilding called Reconstruction. In Massachusetts, where slavery had not been practiced since the Revolutionary War, a small population of African Americans had lived for several generations. They were free citizens and did not suffer the same level of organized discrimination as African Americans faced in the South. Still, most white people in New England did not consider black people their equals.

When William was two years old, his father deserted the family, and William never saw him again. As a toddler, William lived with his mother at his grandparents' farmhouse on the outskirts of town. When he was four years old, his grandfather died. William, his mother, and grandmother moved into the center of Great Barrington, and his mother worked as a maid.[2]

After William entered school, it did not take long for him to attract the attention of adults and other students. He learned quickly and did well in a variety of subjects. William made friends easily. Most were white children because the town had few black families. As a young child, William was not aware of racism.

"I had, as a child, almost no experience of segregation or color discrimination," he later wrote. "My schoolmates were invariably white; I joined quite naturally all games, excursions, church festivals; recreations like coasting, swimming, hiking and games. I was in

Du Bois, age four or five. As a young child in Great Barrington, Massachusetts, William was not aware of racism.

and out of the homes of nearly all my mates, and ate and played with them. I was as a boy long unconscious of color discrimination in any obvious and specific way."[3]

After his grandmother died in 1875, William and his mother moved two more times. For a while, they shared a small, run-down home with another family.[4] When William was twelve, they settled in a small house within sight of the river that ran through town. The house had no electricity or plumbing, which was not unusual in those days. But it was larger than their previous home, and for the first time, William had a room of his own.[5] Although they lived alone, several aunts and cousins also lived in the area.

William and his mother never had much money. Then, when his mother suffered a stroke, she became partially disabled. She walked with a limp and lost most of the use of one hand. Because of her poor health, she could no longer work full-time. But compared with most of his friends, William did not feel unusually poor. "Living was cheap and there was little real poverty," he recalled.[6] People grew much of their own fruit and vegetables, and other food was not expensive.

When he entered high school, William continued to do well with his studies. The principal recognized his talent and encouraged him to study subjects that would prepare him for college. So William took difficult classes such as algebra, geometry, Latin, and

Greek. He also followed the usual pursuits of teens at the time. This included exploring caves, swimming, and playing baseball.

From an early age, William showed a passion for books. During the fall of his second year in high school, he spotted a five-volume edition of Thomas Macaulay's *History of England* displayed in a store window. He did not have enough money to buy it, but he wanted it badly. So he worked out a deal with the store owner to pay in installments of 25 cents a week. After several months, the books were his.

Growing up in a single-parent family, William learned self-reliance. He did what he could to earn money, working at different jobs when he was not in school. One of the hardest was shoveling coal to be used for heating. Another was splitting wood for fireplaces. In the summer, he mowed lawns. He also sold tea and took on a job selling newspapers. All through high school, he worked after school and on Saturdays. But he was eager to bring in money for his mother and himself, and he did not mind working.[7]

Along with these jobs, William at an early age became a writer. He helped edit a high school newspaper and began writing about news of his town for the *Springfield Republican* newspaper. He also wrote articles for the *New York Globe*, a weekly newspaper catering to African-American readers that wanted contributions from writers outside New York.

Many experiences had a lasting effect on William during his youth. One memorable event was the chance to meet his paternal grandfather, Alexander Du Bois, for the first time. The family had not heard from William's grandfather in years. When his grandfather's new wife invited William to come for a visit, he traveled to New Bedford, Massachusetts, in the summer of 1883. He was impressed with his grandfather's elegance and good manners.[8]

On the return trip, he attended a large picnic in Rhode Island. More than three thousand African Americans from a variety of communities in the region were there. This was the first time William had ever been around large numbers of black people. His hometown of Great Barrington had fewer than fifty African Americans. Du Bois was struck by the diversity of people he met. "I was astonished and inspired," he said.[9]

In 1884, Du Bois graduated from high school. He was the only African American in a class of thirteen students. At graduation, he gave a speech on Wendell Phillips, a New Englander who had tried to help abolish slavery.

Du Bois planned to go to college, but he was not able to attend immediately after finishing high school. His mother's health had gotten worse, so he stayed in Great Barrington. He worked to help support the two of them and to save money for college. He worked as

The first and last pages of a letter that fifteen-year-old William wrote to his mother during a visit to his grandfather's home in 1883.

a timekeeper on a construction project, handing out pay envelopes and doing paperwork, for which he earned one dollar a day.[10]

Then in 1885, Du Bois's life changed drastically. In March, his mother died suddenly of another stroke. Since his infancy, when his father had left the family, Du Bois and his mother had relied on each other for emotional as well as economic support. Now he was virtually alone in the world. For a while he lived with an aunt. He made plans to go away to college. He knew, though, that lack of money would be a problem.

Fortunately for Du Bois, several members of the community recognized his potential. A local minister, the Reverend C. C. Painter, was convinced that Du Bois belonged in college. He organized a fund-raising campaign with several churches to come up with money for Du Bois's education. These efforts brought in $100, a large sum at the time.

With Painter's help, Du Bois enrolled at Fisk University in Nashville, Tennessee. In the fall of 1885, he boarded a train and headed south. Great Barrington had been a good place to grow up. But now it was time to move on.

3

COLLEGE WHIZ

u Bois entered Fisk University in the fall of 1885. When he left Great Barrington, he took with him a strong sense of morality, a talent for writing, and a love of learning.[1]

Du Bois's high school training had been more advanced than the typical high school education offered in the 1880s. As a result, seventeen-year-old Du Bois began his Fisk studies as a sophomore rather than starting as a freshman.[2]

When Du Bois arrived in Nashville, he was struck by the differences in cultural and racial attitudes.[3] He had grown up in a northern state where the black population was small, and where most of his fellow students and neighbors were white. At Fisk University, which had been founded less than twenty years earlier as a school for former slaves, almost all the students were African Americans. Most came from the South. People spoke differently, with Du Bois's Massachusetts speech standing out against southern drawls. The foods were different, too. Nothing was quite the same as it had been in New England.

Du Bois got off to a good start at Fisk, but then he became very ill. He contracted typhoid fever, a common disease of the time that was often fatal, and he nearly died. Once his health problems were behind him, Du Bois took full advantage of his time at Fisk. He made friends and studied hard. His classes included chemistry, physics, Latin, Greek, and literature. He sang with the college's Mozart Society. He also joined a church connected with the school.

Du Bois became active in several other areas, too. He developed a close friendship with another student, Thomas Calloway. Du Bois became editor of the school newspaper, *The Herald*, and Calloway served as business manager. The two also worked together to raise money to build a gym. Du Bois enjoyed the environment at Fisk. "Our University is very pleasantly situated overlooking the city," he said, "and the family life is very pleasant indeed. Some mornings as I look about upon the two or three hundred of my

In 1885, Du Bois entered Fisk University in Nashville, Tennessee, with great enthusiasm for his studies and campus life.

companions assembled for morning prayers I can hardly realize they are all my people; that this great assembly of youth and intelligence are the representatives of a race which twenty years ago was in bondage."[4]

At the same time, he began to feel that he was not seeing enough of life in the South. After his first year, he decided to teach summer school in rural Tennessee.[5] He taught and lived in log cabins. The experience was an eye-opener. Du Bois was surprised at the living conditions of the people. They had few possessions. Many lived in run-down shacks. Most were poor. They raised their own food and sometimes did not have enough to eat. But they impressed him with their friendly outlook.

In June 1888, Du Bois graduated from Fisk. He was one of five members of the graduating class. He gave a speech on the German leader Otto von Bismarck. Du Bois admired Bismarck because he had unified Germany and was a strong and successful leader.

Although he was pleased with his diploma, it had always been Du Bois's dream to attend Harvard University in Cambridge, Massachusetts. Now he applied to Harvard and was admitted as a junior. This was a common practice at that time for students who had graduated from less prestigious colleges. He was also awarded a grant to help support his studies.

That summer, before entering Harvard, Du Bois

took a temporary job as business manager for a Fisk glee club quartet. He traveled with the group to a resort hotel in Minnesota. There he worked as a busboy. He found the experience humbling because it involved waiting on other people, many of whom looked down on servants.[6] He also arranged concerts for the quartet elsewhere in the Midwest. Each member of the group ended up making about $100 for the summer.

In the fall, Du Bois moved back to Massachusetts to begin his education at Harvard. He rented a room in Cambridge and walked to classes on the Harvard campus. He studied subjects such as economics, history, philosophy, geology, and chemistry. He especially liked history. His professors included the famous philosophers William James and George Santayana. Du Bois did well in class and made good grades. He also earned a scholarship in addition to the original grant.

At Harvard, Du Bois gained important knowledge for his future work as a professor and researcher. Going to college meant more to him than simply earning a degree. He was fascinated by his courses. He learned about history. He studied the beliefs of major philosophers. He found that understanding social problems was a complex process. It meant gathering and studying information the way a scientist studies laboratory data.[7]

Du Bois had plenty of questions. Why were African

Americans treated differently from those with ancestors from Europe? What events had supported the growth of slavery and later led to its end? What could be done to bring greater equality for all? He pondered such questions and used them as ideas for papers and speeches. When he selected courses, his choices were based in part on how the subject material would help him understand the social order of things.[8]

One of Du Bois's greatest talents was public speaking. He felt comfortable appearing before groups and continued to sharpen his speaking skills while in college. He took second place in a speech contest and raised money by giving lectures and readings for church groups. Du Bois was also interested in the subject of leadership. He read about world leaders. He studied the generals and political leaders of the Civil War. He analyzed just what made a leader successful.

Du Bois was not the only African-American student at Harvard, but he was one of just a few. Although he did well in his classes, he felt he did not fit in socially. When he tried to join the glee club, he was turned away. Du Bois believed the reason was race, not a lack of talent.[9]

He felt out of place at most social events. At one function, a woman insisted that he must be a waiter. She assumed that a young black man would not be socializing with white people.

Faced with this kind of treatment, Du Bois began

spending his free time within the African-American community of Boston. He attended church and went to plays and concerts. He also turned some of the essays he wrote at Harvard into articles for a weekly black newspaper, *The Courant*. He began dating a young woman named Maud Cuney. They considered marriage, but she ended up marrying another man.

In the spring of 1890, Du Bois graduated from Harvard with a bachelor's degree in philosophy. He graduated cum laude (with honors) and was one of six students selected to give speeches at graduation. As his subject he chose Confederate president Jefferson Davis. The Confederacy consisted of southern states that had attempted to break off from the rest of the United States during the Civil War. Du Bois felt that by speaking about Davis, he could call attention to the problems caused by slavery.[10] He was quite a hit. His speech earned praise for its fairness and for the stylish way he delivered it.[11]

Earning a degree from Harvard was a big accomplishment, but Du Bois was not satisfied to stop his education at that point. He dreamed of going on to graduate school and becoming a teacher. Graduate study has become routine today, but it was much less common one hundred years ago. Most people did not attend college at all, let alone seek master's or doctoral degrees. For minority students, such goals were almost unheard of.

Du Bois, far right, graduated with honors from Harvard University. He was one of six students chosen to speak at the graduation ceremony.

But Du Bois was not an ordinary student. He applied to graduate school at Harvard. Not only was he accepted, he received a fellowship to support his studies. At the graduate level, Du Bois studied history and political science. He also took courses in what would later be recognized as the field of sociology. Du Bois did very well in his studies, and his fellowship was renewed for a second year. Du Bois earned his master's degree in history in 1892. He decided he would like to teach in a college.

That fall, Du Bois was selected to make a presentation to the American Historical Association. This was a major accomplishment. He was invited to attend the group's meeting in Washington, D.C., where he spoke on laws affecting slavery. A New York newspaper reported that his was one of the three best papers presented.[12]

At this stage of his life, Du Bois very much wanted to study in Europe. He had long wanted to see more of the world. He also hoped for the chance to study under some of Europe's outstanding professors and to prepare for his career as a college professor. But he did not have the money to go overseas.

As usual, Du Bois did not let a lack of funds stop him. After several efforts, he obtained a grant and a loan to pay for his studies. He went to Europe in August 1892 and traveled in Holland and Germany. Later that fall, he enrolled at Friedrich Wilhelm

University in Berlin, also known as the University of Berlin. The German he had learned at Fisk proved helpful. His course work included history, economics, political economy, and politics.

Along with going to school, Du Bois traveled to other countries, including France, Austria, Hungary, and Italy. He also made friends and expanded his view of the world. He learned that black people faced less discrimination in Europe than in the United States.

Du Bois turned twenty-five years old on February 23, 1893. This was a special day in his life, and he spent it alone. He held a private celebration in which he meditated on the meaning of his life and his plans for the future. He felt that it was his destiny to take on a leader's role. That night, he wrote that he wondered whether he was "a genius or a fool," but that he would "take the world that the Unknown lay in my hands and work for the rise of the Negro people, taking for granted that their best development means the best development of the world."[13]

With this kind of thinking, Du Bois set himself apart from many of his peers. Not only did he foresee his own role as an important leader, but he also recognized that the fate of people in America was connected with that of the citizens of other nations. That belief is common today, but early in the twentieth century it represented creative thinking, especially in the area of race relations. Then, as later in life, Du Bois had his own original way of thinking.

In the spring of 1894, Du Bois ended his European travels. Although he had completed his studies at Friedrich Wilhelm University, school officials refused to grant him a doctorate. They said he had not spent enough time in Germany and did not meet the school's residency requirements. Still, Du Bois had benefited greatly from the chance to study under noted professors at a major European university.

Short on cash as usual, Du Bois then headed back to the United States. He traveled in steerage, the part of the ship reserved for the lowest-paying passengers. Returning to Great Barrington, he visited family and began looking for a college teaching job. Studying in Europe had been a grand experience. Now it was time to put his academic training into practice.

4

SCHOLAR AND PROFESSOR

etting started in one's chosen career is often difficult. As a graduate student, Du Bois had planned to teach in college once he completed his studies. But his first efforts to land a teaching job ended in disappointment. Even though he applied to several schools, it appeared at first that no one would hire him. His application to teach at Howard University in Washington, D.C., was turned down. The same response came from Fisk. Other schools also rejected his applications.

Finally, Du Bois received a job offer. Ohio's Wilberforce University wanted him to teach Greek,

Latin, English, and German. The university was not as well known as some of the other African-American colleges of the time, but Wilberforce offered Du Bois the chance to get his teaching career started. He accepted the offer.

After agreeing to go to Wilberforce, Du Bois received an offer to teach at Missouri's Lincoln Institute. He was also offered a position at Tuskegee Institute in Alabama. But he felt obligated to honor his original commitment, and went on to Wilberforce.[1] Du Bois began his college teaching career in the fall of 1894.

Although he was glad to have a job, Du Bois found that the Ohio college did not offer the kind of environment he had hoped for. The school had little money to support research or other efforts. It was also very conservative in the areas of politics and religion. Prayer revival meetings were common on campus.[2]

For Du Bois, one of the highlights of this time was completing the requirements for his doctor of philosophy degree from Harvard. In 1895, during his first year at Wilberforce, Du Bois finished the book-length report known as a doctoral dissertation. He then received his Ph.D. in history from Harvard. He was the first African American to earn a doctorate from this famous university in its more than 250-year history.

Of course, life is more than work, and Du Bois's personal life also moved forward. He fell in love with a student named Nina Gomer. On May 12, 1896, the two were married. The wedding took place in Cedar Rapids, Iowa, where her family lived. The happy couple returned to campus and moved into a two-room apartment in a men's dormitory.

Du Bois's doctoral dissertation on the African slave trade was published that same year. Because it revealed a wealth of details about slavery never before published, it has been called one of the most important dissertations ever produced in any American university.[3]

The publication of this dissertation highlighted Du Bois's skills as a researcher. When he was offered a short-term position at the University of Pennsylvania to study the sociology of African-American residents of Philadelphia, he readily accepted.

In the fall of 1896, William and Nina Du Bois moved to Philadelphia. They took a one-room apartment above a cafeteria at 700 Lombard Street. This area of the city included slums with run-down buildings. Robberies and other crimes were common. But instead of feeling threatened, Du Bois was excited. Here was a chance to apply the research skills he had learned in college.[4]

Du Bois conducted interviews in more than twenty-five hundred households. He talked to thousands of people. He studied some fifteen thousand documents. He compiled statistics about employment, education, and other matters.

Du Bois was the first African American to earn a Ph.D. degree from Harvard University.

In another project, Du Bois helped start a new group known as the American Negro Academy. It was founded by Alexander Crummel, an Episcopalian minister. Members included Du Bois, the poet Paul Laurence Dunbar, and Kelly Miller, a Howard University philosopher. At the group's first full meeting in March 1897, Du Bois gave a talk against racism that became famous among civil rights activists. It was published later that year as a pamphlet, "The Conservation of Races."

By the spring of 1898, the Philadelphia study was finished. It profiled the economic and social conditions of the African-American community. This was an important accomplishment for Du Bois, for it helped establish his reputation as a researcher. It also helped pave the way for other projects of this type. Today, some scholars point to Du Bois's work in Philadelphia as the "beginning of American sociology."[5] Based on field research in which people's social conditions were examined, it served as an example for later sociologists.

Now it was time for Du Bois to find a permanent job. He accepted a position teaching history and economics at Atlanta University in Georgia. This would take him once again to the South, where slavery was still a recent memory. Before moving to Georgia, he spent the summer in Farmville, Virginia, studying the social and economic conditions of African-American families in a small southern town.

The move to Atlanta marked a major new phase in Du Bois's life. For the first time, he held a teaching job that he did not regard as temporary. He could settle into a new life and devote himself to teaching, writing, and research. He could also continue his work in civil rights. Throughout his life, Du Bois's work consisted of a combination of efforts. At any one time this might include teaching, writing, doing research, traveling, giving speeches, and meeting with other social activists.

W. E. B. Du Bois was also a scholar. He wrote articles for scholarly journals, attended academic conferences, made presentations, and published books. As a scholar, Du Bois broke new ground. He was one of the first people to use research as a tool for understanding the social situations experienced by African Americans. He did not simply accept information at face value; instead he gathered and analyzed data and used the information he gained as a tool for greater understanding.[6] For example, Du Bois studied the educational levels of African Americans. He analyzed information about wages. He collected details about various occupations.

One of his roles was to coordinate conferences on the problems of African Americans who lived in cities. He also started a huge research project made up of a series of studies about the lives of African Americans. Using interviews and questionnaires, Du Bois, an assistant, and a host of volunteers gathered a great deal of information. Then they issued reports on topics such as business, health, crime, education, family life, and other subjects, all from the viewpoint of African Americans.[7]

Du Bois's work as a researcher had far-reaching results. He was among the first to study the sociology of African Americans and to have the results of extensive research published. He also served as a role model for other African-American scholars.

At the same time, living in Georgia exposed Du Bois as never before to the ugliness of racial segregation. He had experienced some discrimination in earlier years, first in his native Massachusetts and later as a college student in Tennessee. But Georgia was part of the Deep South. Slavery had been a fixture of life in the state for generations.

People still remembered the days of slavery. Many who had fought for the Confederacy during the Civil War were still alive to speak of their exploits. Many black Americans who had been slaves or whose parents had been enslaved still lived in the South, as did white people who had owned them.

For most Georgians, African Americans were viewed as an inferior group. They were expected not only to live separately but to accept a life with fewer rights than white citizens. They had to sit in separate streetcars, use separate rest rooms, and in all facets of their lives defer to the white majority. Unfortunately, this separatism was all legal at the time. Laws known as "Jim Crow" laws kept the races apart and limited the rights of minorities.

Du Bois understood that this was a way of life in the South, but he resented it deeply. To show his feelings, he tried to avoid race-based restrictions. If concerts or plays were held only for segregated audiences, he refused to attend them. Instead of riding in segregated streetcars, he walked or rode in a horse-drawn carriage.

In October 1897, William and Nina Du Bois became parents for the first time with the birth of their son. They named him Burghardt Gomer Du Bois, using names from both sides of the family.

In 1898, Du Bois returned to Fisk to speak at graduation. His speech, "Careers Open to College-Bred Negroes," challenged graduates to do what they could to develop the African-American community. He urged them to become professionals, merchants, farmers who would use scientific techniques, and leaders of industry.[8]

Although Du Bois found his work as a sociologist rewarding, events at the time prompted him to expand his work in other directions. One incident that energized him was a criminal case in 1899 involving Sam

Nina and W. E. B. Du Bois and their son, Burghardt.

Hose, a poor African American from Georgia who was accused of murdering a white farmer. The case attracted widespread attention. Du Bois wrote a statement in which he argued for a fair trial. He was on his way to take it to an Atlanta newspaper editor when he learned that Hose had been lynched—hanged and then burned. It was said that people fought over pieces of his body for souvenirs.

The atrocity stunned Du Bois. Recalling it later, he wrote: ". . . one could not be a calm, cool and detached scientist while Negroes were lynched, murdered and starved."[9] Sadly, he realized that as outrageous as the Hose lynching was, it was not a unique occurrence. Too often, African Americans suffered brutal treatment based on racial hatred. Even when they were not the victims of violence, they were often the target of verbal abuse and other mistreatment.

Du Bois became more outspoken than ever. He spoke out against a proposed law that would take away the voting rights of black residents of Georgia. He began writing frequent articles for national magazines such as *The Independent* and *Atlantic Monthly*. Also that year, the results of Du Bois's research conducted in Philadelphia a few years earlier were published as a book, *The Philadelphia Negro*. The study attracted more widespread attention as a book than it had when issued as an academic report, and it helped boost his reputation.

One of the great tragedies of Du Bois's life occurred in 1899. His son, Burghardt, just barely two years old, fell sick with diphtheria, a serious respiratory infection. He died ten days later. Du Bois and his wife were crushed by the loss. The death of their child placed a severe strain on their marriage.[10]

During this time Du Bois became even more active in speaking out against racial injustice. When he attempted to buy a railroad ticket for a sleeping berth but was turned down because of his race, he filed an appeal against the Southern Railway System. After the state reduced funding for schools serving black students, he protested the cuts to the Georgia Legislature. Although neither measure brought success, Du Bois made it clear that African Americans did not have to quietly put up with injustice. In that way, he served as an example for others.

In the summer of 1900, Du Bois traveled to Europe to participate in a world's fair called the Paris Exposition. At this huge event, different nations created displays to welcome the new century. Du Bois designed an exhibit on the economic status of African Americans. He highlighted the accomplishments of African Americans since the Civil War. His exhibit, which included maps, photographs, and models, attracted a great deal of attention and won a grand prize. Du Bois proudly accepted a gold medal for his work.

Du Bois also attended a Pan-African conference in London. Pan-Africanism was a new movement to work for civil rights for African descendants around the world and to recognize their link with Africa. Du Bois wanted to see African colonies freed from rule by European powers. At the conference, he delivered a speech that included one of his most famous statements: "The problem of the twentieth century," he told the audience, "is the problem of the color line."[11] Spoken at the start of a new century, these words pointed to one of the twentieth century's most important issues.

When he returned to the United States, Du Bois turned once again to his teaching and research. That October, Nina and William Du Bois welcomed a baby girl. They named her Nina after her mother but called her by her middle name, Yolande. This turned out to be one of the most stable periods in Du Bois's life. His career kept him busy, and the birth of a daughter helped heal some of the sadness brought by their son's death.[12] The future was full of promise for Du Bois and his family.

5

SOCIAL ACTIVIST

During the early days of his career as a professor, Du Bois considered himself a social scientist, not a civil rights activist. He wanted to study social issues, not crusade against injustice. But as he matured, activism took priority in his life. He continued to write, teach, and conduct research. But increasingly, Du Bois was at the center of a national movement to guarantee civil rights for all.

In his speeches and articles, Du Bois did not shy away from arguments or controversies. Instead, he thrived on them. Often, he became angry at the words or actions of others. Just as often, his own comments angered others.

In 1902, Du Bois received an offer to teach at Tuskegee Institute in Alabama. This school was directed by Booker T. Washington, considered by many to be the most important African-American leader at that time. Du Bois had heard Washington speak but had never met him.

The two men had a meeting to discuss the job offer, which included a hefty increase in salary. But Du Bois felt uncomfortable with the offer. His proposed job duties were vague. Also, he was afraid he would lose some of the independence of thought and action that he treasured.[1] So he declined the offer and remained at Atlanta University.

During this time, Du Bois became known for his concept of the "talented tenth." He believed that an educated elite (roughly 10 percent of the African-American population) should take on a special role as leaders of their people. In an essay published in the 1903 book *The Negro Problem: A Series of Articles by Representative Negroes of Today*, Du Bois argued that college-educated leaders should use their education to help improve life for America's minority population. Members of this elite, he said, should draw upon their "intelligence, broad sympathy, knowledge of the world that was and is, and of the relation of men to it."[2]

This idea caused much debate. Some were inspired by it. Others felt that such a belief caused a gulf between those who attended college and the majority who, in that era, knew they would never be able to go to college.

In many ways, the idea of the "talented tenth" typified Du Bois's style. He was always expressing ideas that some considered brilliant but that offended others. Much of the energy he invested in promoting equal rights was spent interacting with—and often disagreeing with—other leaders. Just as politicians compete to be elected or members of Congress push for their ideas to be passed into law, leaders of social movements often find themselves at odds. With their contrasting visions, they struggle for leadership positions and for influence over group actions. This was the case with Du Bois and other leaders of the civil rights movement. He often clashed with other key figures. Two of the most notable were Booker T. Washington and, later, Marcus Garvey.

Booker T. Washington was Du Bois's main rival for leadership among black Americans at this time. He was an educator who had worked his way out of poverty to become the president of Tuskegee Institute, a school where African-American students learned practical job skills. Washington believed that vocational education in trades such as carpentry, farming, and mechanics was the key to social advancement. Instead of urging African Americans to protest unfair treatment, he encouraged them to go to school. With job skills, he believed, African Americans could earn enough money to gain economic freedom. Then they would at last be in a position to press for civil rights and change.

Washington's approach gained a great deal of support not only from many in the black community but also from much of white America. Whites were happy to have Washington's Tuskegee Institute training a large black workforce. Washington's followers were learning skills, not protesting against the inequality of the races, so his approach was seen as less threatening to the way things were.[3]

A great rivalry developed between Du Bois and Washington. At times it was a bitter one. Du Bois was also an advocate of practical education, but he felt that it was not enough. In his opinion, promoting job skills but failing to speak out against injustice would keep African Americans locked in a permanent underclass. He believed that with academic education, the "talented tenth" of African Americans could fight effectively for the right to vote and to become involved in political decision making. Du Bois wanted some of his people to become leaders for social change.[4]

Du Bois thought that Booker T. Washington held too much power. He believed that Washington tried to control the thinking of other African Americans and wanted to be their only spokesman. "While my leadership was a matter of writing and teaching, the Washington leadership became a matter of organization and money," Du Bois said. "It was what I may call the Tuskegee Machine."[5]

Du Bois recognized what he called Washington's "undisputed leadership of the ten million Negroes in America," but he questioned the fairness of allowing Washington to dictate policy for other black Americans and to represent their interests to political leaders.[6] In his 1903 book, *The Souls of Black Folk*, Du Bois bluntly criticized Booker T. Washington and his tactics:

> His doctrine has tended to make the whites, North and South, shift the burden of the Negro problem to the Negro's shoulders and stand aside as critical and rather pessimistic spectators; when in fact the burden belongs to the nation, and the hands of none of us are clean if we bend not our energies to righting these great wrongs.[7]

The publication of *The Souls of Black Folk* brought increasing attention to Du Bois and his views. It also widened the split between Washington's followers and those who agreed with Du Bois.

More people began to look to Du Bois for leadership and inspiration. In his poem "Credo," published in 1904, Du Bois expressed his belief in God. He also said: "Especially do I believe in the Negro race: in the beauty of its genius, the sweetness of its soul and its strength in that meekness which shall yet inherit this turbulent earth."[8] The poem became widely known. It was often framed and displayed in the homes of African Americans.

Booker T. Washington believed that African Americans should learn practical job skills and work to gain economic freedom. A great rivalry developed between Washington and Du Bois.

"Credo" may not seem unusual today. But early in the twentieth century, African Americans had few pieces of literature that they could call their own. A statement filled with such pride was a major step forward.

In 1905, Du Bois helped organize a group of men to pursue more political and economic rights for African Americans. The group got its start at a meeting held in Canada at Fort Erie, Ontario, in July. About thirty African-American lawyers, editors, physicians, and businessmen attended. The session resulted in the formation of what became known as the Niagara Movement, named after the nearby Niagara Falls.

Du Bois was elected general secretary for the Niagara group. The group set a goal of expanding its membership, with members to come from the educated elite Du Bois had written about. The formation of the Niagara Movement caused a stir among African-American leaders. It was viewed by some as a radical group. Those who followed the more conservative beliefs of Booker T. Washington saw the movement as a threat.[9]

The next year, Du Bois and others met again, at Harper's Ferry, West Virginia. This was the location of John Brown's famous antislavery raid before the Civil War. At the meeting, Du Bois called for an end to the unfair treatment African Americans faced throughout the United States.[10] Foremost, the Niagara Movement

W. E. B. Du Bois (second row, second from right) with other members of the Niagara Movement in 1905. Du Bois helped found this organization, named after nearby Niagara Falls, to fight for economic and political rights for African Americans.

demanded that blacks be given equal rights in all aspects of society and be given the right to vote.

In 1906, Du Bois traveled to Alabama to study the economic situation of rural African Americans, most of whom were farmers. While he was in Alabama, riots broke out in Atlanta. White mobs attacked black residents. Many were beaten, and more than twenty blacks and five or six whites were killed in the fighting.[11]

Du Bois became concerned for his family's safety. He took a train back to Georgia. While on the train, he wrote "A Litany in Atlanta," an emotional appeal for justice, which would be published in the October 11, 1906, *Independent*. On returning to Atlanta, he bought a shotgun and stood guard at his home. For a man of words and ideas, this was a stark example of physical action.

After the Atlanta riots, Du Bois's wife and daughter returned to Massachusetts, where Yolande enrolled in elementary school. Du Bois remained in Atlanta and continued with his work at Atlanta University. Both parents felt that their daughter would be better off in Massachusetts. The move was typical of much of their lives. Du Bois lived where his work took him, and his wife did not always accompany him.

In 1907, Du Bois and some colleagues started a new magazine they called *Horizon*, a monthly "Journal of the Color Line." It provided an outlet for Du Bois to write on a variety of subjects. But financial problems caused the magazine to fold after a few years. (Throughout his life, Du Bois experimented with different literary projects. Some of the magazines he started lasted only a year or two. For about a year starting in December 1905, he had published a paper called *The Weekly Illustrated Moon*. A later example was *The Brownie Book*, a monthly magazine for children begun in 1920 and published through 1921.)

Du Bois continued to be active in the Niagara Movement. A third meeting was held in Boston in 1907. About eight hundred people attended, the largest gathering ever of the organization. Many were attracted by plans to protest African-American exclusion from the events planned that year to celebrate the three-hundredth anniversary of the founding of Jamestown, Virginia. But the protest failed, and the movement stalled.

Another meeting of the Niagara Movement was held in Oberlin, Ohio, in August 1908. Attendance was lower than at previous meetings. It seemed clear that the movement was losing steam and that a new direction was needed.[12]

In 1908, Du Bois gained attention for his stance in the presidential election. Since the Civil War, most African Americans had supported the Republican Party, the party of Abraham Lincoln. But Du Bois endorsed William Jennings Bryan, the Democratic candidate, because he felt Bryan's policies would be better for African Americans. He urged other people to do the same and to support other Democrat candidates. This was considered controversial, but as the years passed, more and more African Americans supported the Democratic Party.

Even though the Niagara Movement was not destined to last, social conditions continued to point to the need for action. A vivid example took place in August 1908. A black man was accused of raping a white woman in Springfield, Illinois. A crowd of angry people stormed the jail where he was held, and a riot broke out. Six people were shot to death, two men were lynched, and scores of people were injured. About two thousand African Americans fled the town. Afterward, white residents boycotted black-owned businesses.[13]

Sadly, this riot was not unique. Race-related violence happened all too often. Most such events took place in the South, but the Springfield riot was in the North. This showed that racial hatred was a national problem, not just a regional one. The Springfield riot was the spark that led to the formation of an interracial movement for civil rights.

In 1909, a new group was formed when a group of white liberals, including New York publisher Oswald Garrison Villard, and black activists, including Du Bois, gathered to discuss problems such as the

Springfield riot of the previous year. It was called the National Negro Committee.

The next year, the National Negro Committee took a new name: the National Association for the Advancement of Colored People (NAACP). Du Bois was the only African American among the five founders of the new group. He was also the first black executive to work with the NAACP's original white leaders.[14]

This was the start of one of the most influential organizations of the twentieth century. Since its formation, the NAACP has played a vital role in protecting and expanding the rights of African Americans. Along with its value to the nation, the NAACP proved of great benefit to Du Bois himself. The chance to serve as one of its leaders gave him a new level of importance. It elevated him from an academic career to a position of national prominence.[15]

The development of the NAACP overlapped the end of the Niagara Movement. One more meeting of this group was held, at Sea Isle City, New Jersey, in 1910. The group was troubled by debts and internal disagreements. In particular, Du Bois and another leader, Monroe Trotter, found it hard to agree on key matters.[16] Thus the movement came to end. But much of its agenda was adopted by the NAACP. With the birth of the NAACP, a new era dawned in the history of American civil rights.

Du Bois at his Atlanta University office in 1909.

6

EDITOR AND
SPOKESMAN

n 1910, Du Bois left his job as professor at Atlanta University to become director of publicity and research for the new NAACP. He moved with his wife and ten-year-old Yolande to New York City, the location of the NAACP headquarters. Du Bois's work with this organization would bring him more visibility than any of his previous work. As the editor of the NAACP's *The Crisis*, Du Bois had a regular vehicle for expressing his views. Along with editing material submitted by others, he could write his own articles and editorials.

Du Bois took full advantage of this opportunity at

The Crisis. He wrote about a variety of subjects. Sometimes he reflected the views of the NAACP, but often the opinions were entirely his own. It was not unusual for him to clash with other NAACP leaders about the contents of *The Crisis*. Frequently, his writing angered readers or the people he criticized. But he believed he had a moral responsibility to speak the truth.[1]

Du Bois wrote fiction, too. He was forty-three years old when his first novel, *The Quest of the Silver Fleece*, was published in 1911. It was the story of several people growing up in the South. It included romance as well as a variety of political ideas and concerns.[2]

In 1911, Du Bois traveled to England to attend the Universal Races Congress. This meeting was one of the first efforts to use science to disprove racist theories. A major theme was that there is no substantial biological difference among people of different races.

At home he continued to speak out about politics. Du Bois was angered by the racial policies of William Howard Taft, who had succeeded Theodore Roosevelt as president. So during the presidential election of 1912, he published an endorsement of Woodrow Wilson, the Democratic nominee for president. Wilson won the election.

In 1913, the original chairman of the NAACP board, Oswald Villard, resigned. He was replaced by

Du Bois's close friend Joel Spingarn. As a result, Du Bois enjoyed even more freedom to speak his mind.[3]

That year, Du Bois wrote a pageant to celebrate the fiftieth anniversary of the end of slavery. Half a century had passed since President Lincoln issued the Emancipation Proclamation in 1863. The pageant, "The Star of Ethiopia," was one of the first public displays of racial pride in African-American history. It was performed in New York and then later in other large cities. Thousands of people attended, and Du Bois was thrilled with its success. The pageant was also enjoyed by whites, many of whom learned new facts about the contributions of African Americans to the nation's history.[4]

In 1914, Du Bois published an editorial supporting women's right to vote. At that time, only men could vote. But a movement was under way to give women suffrage—the right to vote—and Du Bois supported it.

The same spirit prevailed with other public issues. When the 1915 film *Birth of a Nation* opened in theaters, Du Bois helped lead an NAACP campaign against it. He was furious to see the Ku Klux Klan—a racist organization that believes in white supremacy—portrayed in a positive light.[5] When American troops occupied Haiti, Du Bois protested against a large nation unfairly forcing its will on a smaller, weaker country.

In 1915, Booker T. Washington died. Du Bois wrote

Du Bois, front right, and other authors gathered in 1914 to support women's right to vote.

an essay in which he remembered Washington as a leader. While Du Bois praised him for his role as an educational leader, he did not try to hide their strong differences. With his main competitor gone, Du Bois became the major voice for African Americans.

The next year, Du Bois attended a conference in Amenia, New York, sponsored by Joel Spingarn. The purpose was to bring some unity to the factions that had followed Washington and Du Bois. Although disagreements remained, the meeting brought some success. "Probably on account of our meeting, the Negro race was more united and more ready to meet the problems of the world," Du Bois wrote.[6]

This meeting was one of many that Du Bois planned, organized, or attended over the years. Getting together and discussing strategies for action was a frequent way that Du Bois and his peers operated. Assembling in groups, sometimes small and sometimes large, they discussed problems and set goals for future action.

The work of Du Bois and others brought public attention to the way minorities were treated in America. Often, these efforts made white people stop and think about issues they might otherwise have ignored. The efforts also raised the awareness of African Americans of problems they shared as well as the potential for a better future.

For the next few years, Du Bois continued his work

with the NAACP. Then, in 1917, he became seriously ill. He suffered from kidney problems and had two operations. But illness could not slow him down for long.

That year, the United States entered World War I. This was an important war for African Americans. Although they had fought in previous wars, this was the first time in the nation's history that large numbers of African Americans traveled overseas as a part of the military.

The war had started in Europe in 1914. For three years, Americans watched and waited, wondering if the United States would join the fray. In April 1917, Congress declared war on Germany, and American troops were sent to fight in the trenches in Europe. For many African Americans, it was an opportunity to undertake challenging roles with great responsibility. It was a chance to show courage and patriotism. Traveling to Europe also gave them a glimpse of how people lived outside the United States.

Throughout American history, the battlefield has provided a strange combination of hardship and opportunity for African Americans. Sandwiched around mistreatment as a minority group and the dangers of combat itself has been the chance to break out of old restrictions. By showing courage and ability, black Americans could move past the stereotypes held by whites. Such was the hope of many African

Americans who joined the armed forces during World War I.

Du Bois believed it was important that African Americans serve in the military or work in industries supporting the war. At age forty-nine, he was too old for combat, but he became involved in war issues. As an African-American leader, he felt responsible for supporting the interests of the black men who joined the mostly white military. One point of dispute was military training. Du Bois felt that black officers should have their own training programs and facilities. He wanted to make sure they were treated fairly.

Meanwhile, a serious problem on the home front was the continuing specter of racial violence. As white men went off to fight in the war, their jobs were often filled by black workers. Whites felt threatened, fearing that blacks were moving into their neighborhoods and taking their jobs. In East St. Louis, a huge riot broke out in July 1917 when a white mob invaded the black community. Fighting lasted for several days. White rioters roamed black neighborhoods. People fought in the streets. The night sky was bright with the light of burning houses. Scores of people were killed, most of them African Americans. More than six thousand people lost their homes, and much property was damaged.

Du Bois went to St. Louis and investigated the causes of the riot. He and staff member Martha Gruening interviewed survivors and city officials. They completed an extensive report, which was later published in *The Crisis*. Later that month, he joined thousands of others who staged a major demonstration. Marching silently down the streets of New York City, they carried signs protesting the violent treatment of African Americans. The parade was one of the earliest high-profile civil rights protests in America.[7]

Du Bois continued to speak out against racism in the military. He was offered a commission as an army captain, with an assignment to work in a special unit to deal with race-related problems. After deciding to accept, he wrote in *The Crisis* that while the war lasted, it was best to "forget our special grievances" and to "close ranks with our own white fellow citizens and the allied nations that are fighting for democracy."[8]

Du Bois's article angered many people. Some other leaders disagreed with his stance. In response to the controversy, the government withdrew its offer. Instead of serving in the military, Du Bois ended up traveling to France after the war to look into the treatment of African-American troops. He found that black troops had performed well in battle and that the French seemed favorably impressed with them. But he also felt that they had been badly treated by American officers.[9]

The end of the war brought a new order. America's importance as a world leader had grown. Thousands of African Americans had helped win the war. While in

After the terrible St. Louis riot in 1917, thousands marched in New York in the Silent Parade of the NAACP. Du Bois, second row, second from right, helped lead the protest march against violence.

France they were not subjected to the discrimination they faced at home. When they returned to the United States, they were disappointed to find their civil rights were still very limited. Race relations had not improved. Many southern blacks moved to northern states. Especially in the South, lynchings and other violence were common. But many African Americans had expanded their horizons with their experiences overseas. The seeds had been planted for more people to take an active role in working for equality.

7

CIVIL RIGHTS LEADER

hile in France after the end of World War I, Du Bois helped organize a Pan-African Congress. Du Bois and others hoped to bring to public attention the needs of African nations and the potential for people of African descent to work together to achieve common goals. One way to do this was to hold large-scale meetings dubbed "congresses."

Of the civil rights leaders of this century, Du Bois was among the two or three most closely identified with Africa. This was not always a popular position. Many African Americans wanted to distance themselves from the primitive image that Africa often carried in the minds of whites.[1] But Du Bois believed that the need for progress for Africans could not be overlooked. He felt black Americans should support the advancement of black people all over the world.

Du Bois believed that a link to Africa should be maintained. African Americans should remember that continent as a spiritual or political homeland.[2] The concept of Pan-Africanism was a complex one. Because black Americans had all descended from African ancestors, a natural link existed with the continent of Africa. Still, in the same way that many white Americans with ancestors from northern Europe considered themselves Americans rather than Germans or Scandinavians, most black citizens of the United States saw themselves as Americans rather than Africans.

Du Bois largely agreed with this point of view. At the same time, he felt that it was important for Africans and those descended from Africans to work together to promote common interests. Du Bois played a key role when the first Pan-African Congress met in February 1919. Some fifty-seven delegates from Africa, Europe, the West Indies, and the United States attended. During the congress, Du Bois was elected executive secretary. He also served as an observer for the NAACP. The delegates passed a resolution seeking protection of Africans living under the colonial rule of European nations.[3]

Other leaders, including Marcus Garvey, also

wanted to see the liberation of Africans from their European colonial rulers.[4] But where Du Bois sought to improve the status of African descendants around the world, Garvey thought that black Americans should return to their origins and relocate to Africa.

Garvey was born in Jamaica in 1887 but spent most of his adult life in the United States. Garvey believed that black Americans would never gain equality in America and that they should move to Africa. He challenged Du Bois's leadership of the African-American community.

Garvey's dynamic, charismatic appeal drew a large number of followers, especially among the poor. He accused Du Bois and his elite "talented tenth" of not meeting the needs of the black masses, and he criticized Du Bois for working with whites at the NAACP. Garvey published a popular black newspaper, the *Negro World*, established a steamship company and other businesses, and raised millions of dollars for his back-to-Africa movement. The conflict between Garvey and Du Bois did not let up until the mid-1920s when Garvey went bankrupt and was arrested for mail fraud. He was convicted, served two years in jail, then was deported to Jamaica. Despite their rivalry, Du Bois acknowledged Garvey's influence on black racial pride.

Du Bois's widespread efforts for his people were not going unrecognized. In 1920, the NAACP honored him with its Spingarn Medal. Since 1914, this

Du Bois believed that black Americans should support the advancement of black people all over the world.

prestigious award had been given annually by the NAACP to an African American of outstanding achievements.

In 1921, another of Du Bois's most important works was published. *Darkwater: Voices from Within the Veil* was a collection of essays. One in particular created controversy because it warned of the possibility of war between the races.

A second Pan-African Congress was held that year. Taking place over a ten-day period, meetings were held in London, Brussels, and Paris. Du Bois attended in all three locations, but resigned as the organization's secretary. A third Pan-African Congress took place in 1923, but Du Bois did not attend all the sessions. Conflict had developed with the French delegates, and Du Bois refused to attend the meetings held in France. At this point, the Pan-African movement was on the decline. Although another congress would be held a few years later in New York, membership was declining, and funds were limited.[5]

In late 1923 and early 1924, Du Bois made his first visit to Africa. Given his keen interest in that continent, this was a very important event in his life. "The spell of Africa is upon me," he wrote. "The ancient witchery of her medicine is burning my drowsy, dreamy blood."[6]

The first place he visited was Liberia, a country founded by former slaves from America in 1822. He also traveled in Guinea, Senegal, and Sierra Leone, a nation established by American blacks who had fought on the side of the British during the American Revolution.[7]

Du Bois was interested in Africa, but his main concern was still affairs in the United States. One measure of Du Bois's influence was the role he played in forcing a college president out of office. In 1924, he became concerned that Fayette McKenzie, then president of Fisk University, was not leading the college in the direction Du Bois thought it should go. The president tended to punish students harshly and, Du Bois believed, gave in too often to the wishes of white segregationists.[8] He was the school's most famous alumnus, so Du Bois's opinion carried a great deal of weight. He insisted that McKenzie be ousted. After a year of debate, Du Bois won out, and the Fisk president was replaced.[9]

Du Bois also remained active as a writer during the 1920s. At that time, a number of African-American writers and intellectuals spurred an excitement in African-American culture. Art and literature were used to show the experience of being black in America. Harlem, in New York City, was the center of this rebirth and blossoming of African-American pride and expression, which was known as the "Harlem Renaissance." Whites, too, were caught up in the excitement. Jazz and blues were all the rage in music. Poets Countee Cullen and Langston Hughes, novelist

Jean Toomer, and many others attracted white as well as black readers.

Du Bois also participated in this thriving cultural movement. Besides encouraging other writers and publishing their work in *The Crisis*, he wrote essays and reviews about literature, music, and drama. His essay on Africa, "The Negro Mind Reaches Out," was published in 1925 in an influential book by scholar Alain Locke, *The New Negro: An Interpretation*.

One of the most controversial aspects of Du Bois's life developed during this period: his interest in communism. In the 1920s, when he first became acquainted with their beliefs, Communists were new on the world scene. They had taken power in the Russian Revolution of 1917 and were still in the early stages of a new experiment in government. In later years, communism became a hated word for most Americans, but in its early days many people were attracted by its stated goal of bringing equality to all.

Du Bois was among those who found communism intriguing. He felt that its basic message was that people should be treated equally, both economically and socially. The actual practice of Communist governments in the Soviet Union, China, and elsewhere never lived up to the hopes of their creators, but early followers were often idealistic.

In 1926, Du Bois was invited to visit the Soviet Union (now the Commonwealth of Independent

States, of which the Russian Federation is the largest republic). During a two-month trip, he visited Moscow, Leningrad, and several other cities. He also stopped in Germany, Turkey, Greece, and Italy. Du Bois was impressed with what the Soviets had accomplished. On his return to the United States, he wrote an article for *The Crisis* praising the results of the Russian Revolution.[10]

During the next few years, Du Bois combined work at the NAACP with writing. He sponsored a Harlem theater group that presented plays about African-American men and women. He also continued to write novels and other works. Du Bois's second novel, *Dark Princess*, was published in 1928. It is the story of an Indian princess and a black American who fall in love. More than just a romance, it contains far-reaching commentary on politics and social issues.

In 1928, Du Bois's daughter, Yolande, married the poet Countee Cullen. The huge, extravagant wedding celebration was the big social event of the season in Harlem. Du Bois was well known by then. Living in New York City, writing for national publications, and traveling often to attend meetings or make speeches, Du Bois had developed a reputation as an intelligent, outspoken leader.

In 1930, Du Bois was awarded an honorary doctor of laws degree by Howard University in Washington, D.C. He also gave the commencement address.

In his speech, "Education and Work," he urged African-American colleges to help build economic power for the black community by giving students the educational background they needed to succeed.[11]

The early 1930s included some difficult times for America and for Du Bois personally. The nation was mired in the Great Depression. Millions of people were unemployed. African Americans, many of whom were already at the low end of the economic spectrum, suffered even more than the population as a whole.

At the same time, Du Bois was experiencing problems of his own. *The Crisis* was losing money, and that created conflict between Du Bois and other leaders of the NAACP.[12] Du Bois argued with them about how to handle the NAACP's money problem. He also tried to change the way officers of the NAACP were selected. He engaged in a verbal battle with the executive secretary of the NAACP, Walter White. Most of the group's leaders backed White. Du Bois then resigned from the organization.[13]

Some scholars feel that Du Bois was never again as influential as he had been before this series of events. He still had his admirers, and in many ways stood as a symbol for other African Americans. But his views did not make him popular.

That year, 1934, Du Bois returned once again to the faculty of Atlanta University. His wife, Nina, did not move with him to Atlanta. She did not want to return to the city where her firstborn child had died. Instead she went to Baltimore, where their daughter, now divorced, was living.

Some people viewed Du Bois's move back to Atlanta University as a kind of retirement. They thought he would live quietly and dabble in academic affairs. But Du Bois had no such plans. He was as energetic as ever and plunged into a heavy work schedule.[14]

Sometimes it is hard to understand Du Bois. One reason is that he did so many things. He was not just a writer or professor. He was not just a sociologist or civil rights activist. He was all of these, and more. When he returned to Atlanta, his job at the university allowed him to stay involved with all his interests. Even if he was no longer employed by the NAACP, he could express his ideas while teaching and attending conferences. He could contribute to magazines and newspapers, write books, and conduct research projects.

That is exactly what Du Bois did. He taught several courses, including one on communism. Half of his teaching load was at the graduate level, where he enjoyed working closely with students. He was proud that some went on to become social workers or college teachers.[15] He also made plans to revive the old Atlanta University conferences he had sponsored when he worked there before going to the NAACP.

During this period, Du Bois was especially prolific. He wrote scores of research studies, essays, magazine articles, academic publications, speeches, and lectures. Perhaps his most important work of the time was *Black Reconstruction in America*. Published in 1935, this long, detailed book describes the period in the South following the Civil War.

In 1936, Du Bois visited several European countries, including Germany. That country had changed greatly since Du Bois had studied there as a young man. Dictator Adolf Hitler had risen to power and was building a powerful military. Hitler's Nazi Party had taken away many of the freedoms of citizens. Germany was moving down a warlike path that three years later would lead to World War II.

Du Bois talked about these changes in a weekly column he wrote for the *Pittsburgh Courier*. Among his commentaries, he spoke out against Germany's persecution of Jews and other minorities. This was a courageous act at a time when many people chose to ignore what was happening.

After leaving Germany, Du Bois visited the Soviet Union, China, and Japan. He returned home and turned once again to writing. By now, Du Bois had gained a reputation as a senior statesman within the African-American community. In 1938, the year he turned seventy, Du Bois received a number of honors. Atlanta University and Fisk University both awarded him honorary doctorates, and he was invited to deliver Fisk's commencement address.

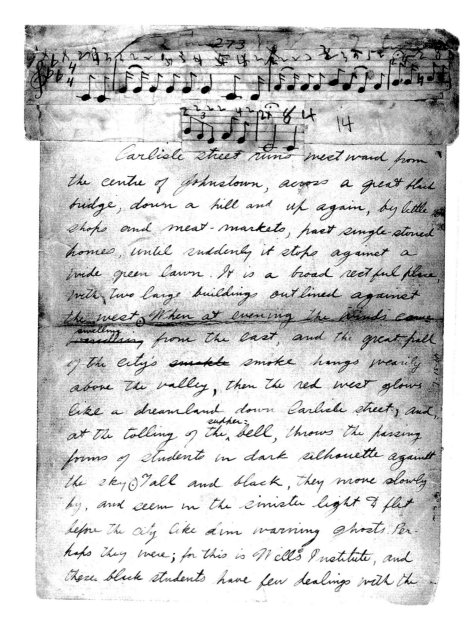

Du Bois was always writing—essays, articles, speeches, and books. This is a page of Du Bois's handwritten narrative from a work in progress.

In honor of Du Bois's birthday, a special celebration was held by Atlanta University, Morehouse College, and Spelman College. For the occasion, Du Bois gave a speech based on his life history, "A Pageant in Seven Decades, 1868–1938."[16]

Du Bois published another book in 1939: *Black Folk, Then and Now*. It was an expanded version of his earlier work, *The Negro*, which had appeared in 1915. *Dusk of Dawn*, an autobiography, followed the next year.

In 1940, Du Bois founded a new magazine focusing on the study of black issues. Called *Pylon*, "a journal of race and culture," it was published four times a year. Du Bois also undertook a major project: studying the educational systems serving African-American students. He visited colleges around the South. He lobbied for more federal funding. He proposed measures to study economic and social conditions.

As it had during much of his life, controversy surrounded Du Bois during his later years at Atlanta University. The school had a new president, and Du Bois disagreed with him on several issues. Du Bois's activism was seen as a source of problems. Some viewed him as a radical from the North. In late 1943, the Board of Trustees forced Du Bois to retire at the end of the school year.

Du Bois was already past the normal retirement age, but this was a heavy blow. He did not feel financially prepared for retirement, and he wanted to continue working. "Without a word of warning I found myself at the age of seventy-six without employment and with less than $5,000 of savings," he recalled later. "Not only was a great plan of scientific work killed at birth, but my own life was thrown into confusion."[17]

The trustees of Atlanta University gave him a year's salary and a pension. Also, both Fisk University and Howard University offered him positions. But Du Bois decided instead to return to the organization where he had worked before: the NAACP.

Du Bois's new job as director of special research for the NAACP began in September 1944. He focused on achieving world peace and making sure that African Americans were included in peace plans.[18]

In the spring of 1945, Du Bois attended an important conference in San Francisco. There a draft was written of a charter for a new organization to be known as the United Nations. Two world wars had been fought since 1914, and the need for an organization dedicated to maintaining peace was obvious. This conference helped create the United Nations and its mission of promoting peace.

Du Bois's role was to help represent the NAACP to the American delegation at the San Francisco conference. But he also held deep feelings about issues that affected the entire world, not just the United States. Chief among these was his opposition to colonialism—the practice in which some countries took over foreign lands and used them for their own purposes. Although the colonizing of America was old news, it was still a problem in Africa, where much of the continent was ruled by European nations. Du Bois urged that the United Nations charter include statements against colonialism. To his disappointment, this did not happen.[19]

Du Bois, as usual, did not give up. In October 1945, he attended another Pan-African Congress. This meeting, the fifth of its kind since 1919, was held in Manchester, England. Du Bois spoke forcefully, and the delegates treated him as an honored elder statesman. The members of the Congress approved resolutions against poverty and colonialism and for the right to organize labor unions.[20]

Du Bois worked for several more years, pursuing such issues and speaking out against racism. But once again, he upset a number of leaders within the NAACP. His views on Pan-Africanism were more radical than those of most members of the organization. Some NAACP leaders feared that because of Du Bois, the group would get a bad reputation as a "Communist" organization.[21]

Du Bois also supported the 1948 campaign of Henry Wallace, a former vice president who ran as a third-party presidential candidate for the liberal Progressive Party. Du Bois angered Walter White, the head of the NAACP, by becoming too involved in the campaign. An NAACP policy limited the political activity of NAACP officers. Staff members were forbidden to endorse candidates. Then, when Du Bois wrote a critical memo that became public in September 1948, he was fired by the NAACP.[22]

This might have been a crushing blow for someone else, especially considering that Du Bois was now eighty years old. Certainly, he was saddened by these events. But once again, he rebounded. His old friend Paul Robeson, the singer, actor, and fellow civil rights leader with controversial political views, asked Du Bois to serve as honorary vice chairman of his Council of African Affairs, a fund-raising and educational organization. The job paid no salary, but it provided office space and secretarial help.[23]

Du Bois accepted. The position would give him a means to continue writing and speaking out on what he believed. He was like a tough old boxer; you could bring him down, but you could never knock him out.

8

MAN OF
CONTROVERSY

N ot long after World War II, America entered into what became known as the Cold War between Communist and non-Communist countries. The United States and its democratic allies were in intense competition with the Soviet Union and other Communist nations. Increasingly, communism was seen by most Americans as an evil force that posed a major threat to the world. In Communist countries, people lacked the individual freedom they enjoyed in democracies. Many Americans believed that Communists wanted to spread their power over the entire world, using spies to overtake democratic nations from within.

Anti-Communist feelings reached a peak in the early 1950s when Senator Joseph McCarthy conducted a series of hearings on what he called "un-American" activities. Hundreds of citizens, including large numbers of writers, actors, and other outspoken people, were investigated. Many were charged with being members of the Communist Party or Communist sympathizers. Some people went to jail. Others lost their jobs or were prevented from getting new jobs.

At this time Du Bois was not a member of the Communist Party, but he had been quite open about his support for Communist ideas. This caused conflict with other civil rights leaders. Most Americans, regardless of race, were against communism. Some leaders felt that Du Bois's beliefs might cause others to withdraw their support of civil rights issues.

In 1950, Du Bois became involved in a new organization known as the Peace Information Center. Its purpose was to inform the American public about worldwide efforts related to promoting peace.[1] The Peace Information Center's best-known project was getting people to sign the Stockholm Appeal, an international petition against nuclear weapons. This was a controversial stance. The secretary of state claimed the petition was really a trick by the Soviet Union.[2] But Du Bois defended the work of the center and continued his association with it.

In July 1950, Du Bois's wife, Nina, died in

Baltimore. After suffering a series of strokes, she had been an invalid for the last few years of her life. The pair had been married for fifty-three years, although much of that time had been spent apart. She was buried in Great Barrington, next to their son, Burghardt. Du Bois wrote a loving tribute to Nina, which was published in the *Chicago Globe*.[3]

A conservative political tide was sweeping the nation, and it was to have a major impact on Du Bois. In August, he was notified by the United States government that he must register as an agent of a foreign government. He brushed this off with a response that the Peace Information Center was not representing a foreign government; it was representing peace.

Meanwhile, he put his energies into a political campaign. The American Labor Party asked Du Bois to run for one of New York's two seats in the United States Senate. Du Bois knew from the start that he had no chance of winning. He had never held political office. The party he represented was not a major one. Plus, it was highly unlikely that an African American could be elected to the Senate. But Du Bois's candidacy would help bring votes to the campaign of Congressman Vito Marcantonio, who was running for reelection. Also, a political campaign would give Du Bois a chance to present his views to a wide audience.[4]

So Du Bois campaigned actively in the fall of 1950. He made speeches both in person and on the radio.

Singer/political activist Paul Robeson, left, shows his support for American Labor Party candidates W. E. B. Du Bois, running for Senate, and Vito Marcantonio, campaigning for reelection to Congress.

When the election was held, he did surprisingly well considering his late entry into the campaign and the fact that he represented a fringe party. When the results were tabulated, he received almost 13 percent of the vote in Harlem and 4 percent of the vote of the entire state of New York.[5]

That winter, his luck changed for the worse, and Du Bois had to face one of the biggest challenges of his life. He and four associates were arrested and charged with breaking a law known as the Foreign Agents Registration Act. This law required any American who represented a foreign government to register with the United States government. Du Bois had not complied with the government's request that he register as a foreign agent. Because of his work with the Peace Information Center, Du Bois was charged with being a Soviet agent.

In a humiliating chain of events, Du Bois was arrested, searched, and handcuffed. Then he was released on bail. If convicted, he faced up to five years in prison and a fine of $10,000.[6]

During his long life, Du Bois had made many acquaintances, although he felt he had few truly close friends. Perhaps the closest of all was Shirley Graham, a prominent civil rights activist in her own right, who was also a teacher and a writer. They had first met decades earlier. She admired him greatly, and they began corresponding. As time passed, they had become close friends as well as political allies.

"Shirley Graham," Du Bois wrote, "with her beautiful martyr complex, finally persuaded herself that I needed her help and companionship, as I certainly did; so we decided to get married a few days after my next birthday, when I would be eighty-three years old."[7]

With Du Bois facing criminal charges and the chance of being jailed, it became clear that one way to make certain Shirley Graham could visit him if he went to jail would be to marry. They moved up the date and were married on February 14, 1951. One result of this marriage was that Du Bois gained a son. Shirley had a son from a previous marriage, David Graham. Du Bois came to regard him as his own son and adopted him, giving him the Du Bois name.

Over the next nine months, Du Bois and his supporters fought a public relations campaign against the charges. He crossed the country, making speeches and raising money for a legal defense fund. Du Bois's supposed crime was based on ideas rather than some other type of illegal activity. He certainly was not a threat to the security of the United States. He was not a traitor. He was not about to topple the government. But by associating himself with Communist ideas, he sparked the fear that the word *Communist* prompted during the 1950s.

In 1951, eighty-three-year-old Du Bois married Shirley Graham, a teacher, writer, and civil rights activist.

The experience was a scary one for Du Bois. Recalling it later, he wrote: "I have faced during my life many unpleasant experiences: the growl of a mob; the personal threat of murder; the scowling distaste of an audience. But nothing has so cowed me as that day, November 8, 1951, when I took my seat in a Washington courtroom as an indicted criminal."[8]

The trial got under way, and for a while Du Bois worried that he would be found guilty. But as the testimony continued, the judge came to believe that the government failed to prove its case that the Peace Information Center was distributing Communist literature. A jury had been assembled, but it never had to make a decision. The judge acquitted Du Bois and the others. They were innocent and free to go.

Although Du Bois was happy that the trial turned out in his favor, he realized that damage had been done. There had been a great deal of publicity, and much of it centered on Du Bois's Communist sympathies. Still, Du Bois continued to speak out, defending the Soviet Union and attacking what he saw as the government's persecution of Communists.

As a result of the trial and the controversy about his political beliefs, Du Bois lost what remained of his leadership status. He was forever tainted by the experience.[9] After this, many of his friends turned against him. Most American publishers refused to publish his books. Colleges and other groups stopped asking him to make speeches. The NAACP would not let local branches invite Du Bois to visit or speak.[10]

Du Bois found the experience a bitter one. But at the same time, he tried to find a positive side. "The color line was beginning to break," he said. "Negroes were getting recognition as never before. Was not the sacrifice of one man, small payment for this?"[11]

9

EXPATRIATE

fter his trial was over, Du Bois wrote about the experience in another book, *Battle for Peace*. Even in his eighties, he kept active. But Du Bois continued to have problems. He became known more than ever before as a radical. Although most Americans were strongly against communism, Du Bois continued to sympathize with Communist positions. Many people felt he had gone too far.

Du Bois had always traveled widely, but now the United States government put a stop to that. The government refused to renew his passport. The State Department claimed that allowing Du Bois to travel to other countries was not in the national interest of the United States.[1]

Du Bois protested, and the government then changed its stance. If he would sign a statement that he was not a member of the Communist Party, a passport would be issued. But Du Bois would not sign. As always, he believed in sticking to his principles.

In 1953, Josef Stalin died. He was not only the leader of the Soviet Union, America's main rival, but also the idol of most of the world's Communist nations. Although the United States and the Soviet Union were not at war, many Americans considered Stalin an enemy. So when Du Bois wrote a eulogy praising Stalin in the *National Guardian*, he caused more controversy.

The same year, Du Bois campaigned to save the lives of Ethel and Julius Rosenberg. In one of the most famous criminal cases in American history, the two had been found guilty of spying for the Soviet Union. They had been sentenced to die in the electric chair. Du Bois and others tried to prevent their execution, but the Rosenbergs were put to death. At their funeral, he gave an emotional eulogy.

In 1954, one of the most important events in the history of the United States occurred. In a case originating in Kansas known as *Brown* v. *Board of Education*, the United States Supreme Court ruled that it was illegal to segregate public schools. African-American children would no longer be educated in separate schools. Instead, they would have the same educational opportunities as white children. This was a stunning development. Although Du Bois played no direct role in the case, it was the kind of progress he had fought for all his life.[2]

Du Bois remained an outcast in the United States. His social and political views were too controversial and unpopular. Many other countries, however, held him in high esteem. Du Bois was asked to attend the World Youth Festival in Warsaw, Poland. But he was again denied a passport and could not travel to Poland. Protesting the refusal, he wrote to passport officials: "My beliefs are none of your business. I repeat my demand for a passport in accordance with the Constitution of the United States, the laws of the land, and the decision of the courts."[3]

When he was invited to speak in the People's Republic of China in 1956, his lack of passport clearance once again kept him from traveling. The same problem kept him from attending ceremonies in Africa when Ghana became an independent country.[4]

Even within the United States, Du Bois faced restrictions. He planned to speak at a rally held by the American Labor Party on Long Island, New York, but local officials would not allow it because of his identification with Communist ideals.[5]

Despite these problems, Du Bois was not entirely

forgotten. His lifetime of dedication was still recognized by many in the African-American community. He was once again invited as a guest speaker at colleges and other organizations. A bust of Du Bois was displayed at the New York Public Library, and he was the honored guest at its unveiling.

Du Bois also continued to be a successful writer. Over a four-year period beginning in 1957, Du Bois had three books published. They became known as the *Black Flame* trilogy: *The Ordeal of Mansart, Mansart Builds a School,* and *Worlds of Color.* Taken together, they portray the fictional Mansart family from the days of slavery into modern times. They include actual historical events as well as imaginary ones.[6]

In February 1958, Du Bois celebrated his ninetieth birthday. A large crowd of people attended a special ceremony held on March 2 in his honor at the Roosevelt Hotel in New York City. He was also honored with several repeat celebrations over the next few weeks.[7]

More recognition came when Du Bois was named an alumni member of Fisk University's chapter of Phi Beta Kappa. This is one of the nation's most prestigious honor societies. Although it came late in life, the distinction was important for Du Bois.[8]

Later that year, Du Bois's travel problems were at last resolved. The United States Supreme Court ruled that the government could not force a citizen to sign a statement of the type it had demanded from Du Bois

A bust of Du Bois was created in honor of his lifetime dedication to civil rights.

regarding his political beliefs. As a result, he was able to obtain a passport once again.

In August, Du Bois began a world tour. First he traveled to England, France, Belgium, and Holland. Then he visited Czechoslovakia, East Germany, and the Soviet Union.

While in East Germany, he received an honorary doctorate from Humboldt University. This was the same school he had attended as a young man, but its name had been changed from Friedrich Wilhelm University.

While Du Bois was in the Soviet Union, the rigors of travel caught up with him. He had been invited to speak at a conference in Ghana attended by representatives from throughout Africa, but he was too exhausted to travel there. So Shirley Graham Du Bois went to Ghana and gave the speech for him.[9]

In his speech, which was later published, Du Bois urged Africans to avoid becoming financially tied to the United States and other Western nations. This came at a time when the United States and the Soviet Union were competing for influence around the world. One way they did this was by providing money to nations needing help. Du Bois warned Africans not to become dependent on American or European aid.[10]

While in the Soviet Union, Du Bois had a meeting with its leader, Nikita Khrushchev. Then he traveled to China and met with its top leaders, Mao Tse-tung and

Chou En-lai. After visiting the Soviet Union again and traveling to Sweden and England, Du Bois returned to the United States in July 1959. He had been gone nearly a year.

In September, he was awarded the International Lenin Prize. This was a major honor in the Communist world, but most people in the United States did not respect it.

In 1960, Du Bois visited Africa once again. Times were changing, and Africans were gaining more independence. He was an honored guest as the nation of Ghana was established as a republic. Then he traveled to Nigeria, where that nation's first African governor-general was inaugurated.[11]

In the United States, the 1960s were years of racial turmoil. Leaders such as Du Bois had worked for decades to promote civil rights. Now, at last, the push for racial equality took center stage. Another generation of leaders had emerged. Martin Luther King, Jr., and others made speeches and organized protest marches. The civil rights movement reached new heights. At the same time, whites who did not believe in integration bitterly opposed it. This growing social conflict was featured on television, a powerful new medium that brought vivid images of protest and confrontation into American homes.

In 1961, Du Bois's daughter, Yolande, died of a heart attack at age sixty. Her death was a heavy blow, and Du

Bois remarked to his wife that he wished he could have died in her place.[12] She was buried in Great Barrington, Massachusetts, beside her mother and her brother.

That year, Du Bois, age ninety-one, joined the United States Communist Party. After years of controversy regarding his views, he felt it was time to become an official member of the party. His action was, at least in part, a protest against the treatment he had received from the American government.

Du Bois then turned to some work begun years before. He revived his plans to develop an encyclopedia about Africa. After having worked for decades to improve the lot of African Americans, Du Bois felt it was time to take a personal but symbolic step. He decided to leave the United States and live in Africa. He informed the president of Ghana that he would come to Africa and supervise the encyclopedia project from there.[13]

Why did Du Bois move to Africa? The popular belief is that he had given up on his native country, saddened that decades of struggle had still not brought a totally equal society. Discouraged by the way he had been treated and tired of facing resistance, Du Bois felt that leaving the United States might be simpler than staying.

But his feelings were not as bitter as they might appear. He had long wanted to compile an encyclopedia about Africa. Although in rapidly failing health,

Du Bois felt that moving to Africa would give him a chance to work on this huge project. Also, the president of Ghana had long been an admirer of Du Bois and had invited him to come to Africa.[14]

Du Bois turned ninety-five on February 23, 1963. In a fitting tribute, the University of Ghana awarded him an honorary doctorate.

Even in old age, Du Bois did not abandon his passion for equal rights. He followed with great interest the plans being made in the United States for a major civil rights march on Washington, D.C. But on the night before the march, on August 27, 1963, William E. B. Du Bois died.

Du Bois's death attracted worldwide attention. He was known not only in America but also in many other countries around the world. At the great civil rights march on Washington, D.C., some 250,000 people paid tribute to him. Just before the huge group of marchers departed from the Washington Monument, they observed a moment of silence after the announcement of his death.[15]

On August 29, Du Bois was given a state funeral by the government of Ghana. He was buried in Accra, the capital. Following the initial splendor, he was given a simple, dignified burial.[16] Later, his remains were reentombed with a special ceremony and new crypt.

It can be said that with Du Bois's death, an era came to an end. Certainly, few if any leaders played a

Du Bois celebrates his ninety-fifth birthday in 1963 with the president of Ghana, Kwame Nkrumah.

greater role in the long-term development of the American civil rights movement. Even the few who have become more famous, such as Martin Luther King, Jr., acknowledged the debt they owed to Du Bois. He was, without doubt, one of the most influential thinkers in American history.

Dr. King called Du Bois "one of the most remarkable men of our time."[17] In a speech delivered on the one-hundredth anniversary of Du Bois's birth, King said, "Dr. Du Bois the man needs to be remembered today when despair is all too prevalent. In the years he lived and fought, there was far more justification for frustration and hopelessness, and yet his faith in his people never wavered. His love and faith in Negroes permeate every sentence of his writings and every act of his life."[18]

10

INFLUENTIAL THINKER

uring his life and after his death, Du Bois's influence on others was a powerful force. He served as an inspiration for advocates of African-American causes and for generations of scholars and journalists.[1]

Scholar Manning Marable has said that "few intellectuals have done more to shape the twentieth century than W. E. B. Du Bois."[2] In the movement for civil rights in the United States, said Marable, only Frederick Douglass and Martin Luther King were his equal. In his acclaimed biography of Du Bois, scholar David Levering Lewis described him as a legendary figure who was revered by hundreds of thousands of Americans, both black and white.[3]

One feature that distinguished Du Bois from most other civil rights leaders was his extremely long and active life. Du Bois's main rival, Booker T. Washington, died in 1915. Du Bois, only seven years younger, continued as a prominent figure for nearly fifty years after Washington's death.

Few leaders in our history have seen as much change in their lifetimes. Du Bois was born less than five years after the end of the Civil War. There was no radio or television. Automobiles and airplanes were still far in the future. Andrew Johnson, who became president when Abraham Lincoln was shot, was still in office.

By the time Du Bois died, America had fought the Spanish-American War, two world wars, and the Korean War and was becoming involved in Vietnam. The United States had risen to become the world's dominant power. Seventeen presidents had come and gone. Television, motion pictures, jet planes, and other inventions had made their mark. Perhaps most important for African Americans, the civil rights movement was poised for great accomplishments.

A special strength was Du Bois's high level of energy. Historian Herbert Aptheker, a friend for much of his life, commented that Du Bois never really seemed to grow old except at the very end of his long

The W. E. B. Du Bois Library at the University of Massachusetts in
Amherst was named in honor of the great civil rights leader.

life. He recalled watching Du Bois run up the stone steps at Atlanta University when he was sixty because he wanted to see a beautiful view of flowers. He also remembered seeing Du Bois, nearly ninety, sitting on a piano bench and belting out a song with a young child.[4]

Du Bois also played an important role as one of the most accomplished writers of his time. His work included much more than the editorials he wrote for *The Crisis* or the written texts of his many speeches. He wrote novels, poems, scholarly books, essays, magazine articles, thousands of newspaper articles, lectures, and letters. The total is amazing. A list of all his works would take up many pages.

An important work for understanding this complex man is the autobiography written near the end of his life. It is more complete and objective than his earlier autobiographical work. *The Autobiography of W. E. B. Du Bois: A Soliloquy on Viewing My Life from the Last Decade of Its First Century* was published in 1968. In his preface, Herbert Aptheker explains that Du Bois wrote most of the book in 1958 and 1959, and then revised it in 1960. Shortened versions were published in several Communist countries, but the full book did not appear in the United States until after Du Bois's death.[5]

After his death, Du Bois was not forgotten. Those who followed him in the civil rights movement often cited him as a great leader. His written works were included in high school and college English and history courses. Buildings such as the Du Bois Library at the University of Massachusetts were named after him. The United States Postal Service placed his portrait on a postage stamp. Du Bois did not live to fulfill his dream of an encyclopedia of Africa, but one day others would work toward that goal. In 1999, a team of scholars led by Harvard professors Henry Louis Gates, Jr., and Kwame Anthony Appiah published a comprehensive, multimedia CD-ROM, *Encarta Africana*, a history of Africa, African Americans, and the African diaspora—those of African descent settled all around the world.

Most of all, Du Bois continued as a source of inspiration to others. According to Aptheker, there is no outstanding African-American creative figure of the twentieth century who did not, at some point, draw inspiration from the life and work of W. E. B. Du Bois.[6]

Du Bois was dedicated to his work. He always sought to do more and to make things better. In a short piece, "Advice to a Great-Grandson," he wrote that "the satisfaction with your work even at best will never be complete, since nothing on earth can be perfect. The forward pace of the world which you are pushing will be painfully slow. But what of that: the difference between a hundred and a thousand years is

Du Bois was a controversial figure in his time, but he is now recognized as one of the greatest civil rights leaders in history.

less than you now think. But doing what must be done, that is eternal even when it walks with poverty."[7]

How will history judge W. E. B. Du Bois? Scholars often debate such questions. Some have criticized Du Bois because of the radical positions he took. Others have praised him for his brilliant mind and the courage of his convictions.

For decades, Du Bois was the leading voice of African Americans in the struggle for civil rights. He played a major role in helping start the NAACP, one of the most important social-action groups of the twentieth century. He struggled for African independence. He was an accomplished and prolific writer. Perhaps most important, he inspired a whole generation of activists.

Today, African Americans enjoy legal protections that were only a dream in Du Bois's youth. Economically, politically, and socially, African Americans have progressed enormously since Du Bois's time. Problems remain, but the United States is a better place because of the life and work of W. E. B. Du Bois.

CHRONOLOGY

1868—William Edward Burghardt Du Bois is born on February 23 in Great Barrington, Massachusetts.

1884—Graduates from high school.

1888—Earns bachelor's degree from Fisk University.

1890—Receives bachelor's degree from Harvard University.

1892—Earns master's degree from Harvard University; begins studies at Friedrich Wilhelm University in Berlin, Germany.

1894—Teaches at Wilberforce University.

1895—Becomes the first African American to receive a Ph.D. from Harvard University.

1896—Marries Nina Gomer; studies the sociology of African-American residents of Philadelphia.

1897—Takes job at Atlanta University; son, Burghardt, is born.

1899—Burghardt dies.

1900—Daughter, Nina Yolande, is born.

1903—Publication of *The Souls of Black Folk*.

1905—Helps form the Niagara Movement.

1909—Helps found the National Negro Committee, which in 1910 becomes the National Association for the Advancement of Colored People (NAACP).

1910—Begins working for the NAACP and serving on its board; founds and edits *The Crisis*.

1911—*Quest of the Silver Fleece*, a novel, is published.

1913—Writes pageant, "The Star of Ethiopia."

1917—Works for better treatment of African-American troops in World War I.

1919—Plays key role in first Pan-African Congress.

1920—Is awarded the Spingarn Medal by the NAACP.

1921—Collection of essays, *Darkwater: Voices from Within the Veil*, is published.

1928—Publication of novel *Dark Princess*.

1934—Resigns from the NAACP; returns to Atlanta University.

1935—Publication of *Black Reconstruction* in America.

1936—Visits Hitler's Germany and other countries.

1938—Receives two honorary doctorates; delivers autobiographical address at a special celebration held in honor of his birthday.

1944—Retires from Atlanta University; returns to employment with NAACP.

1948—Fired by the NAACP.

1950—Wife, Nina, dies; runs for senator from New York.

1951—Marries Shirley Graham; tried and found innocent of acting as a foreign agent.

1952—Publication of *Battle for Peace*.

1959—Travels internationally; meets with leaders of Soviet Union and China.

1958 —Writes *The Autobiography of W. E. B. Du Bois: A*
–1960 *Soliloquy on Viewing My Life from the Last Decade of Its First Century,* which is not published until 1968.

1961—Joins the Communist Party; daughter, Yolande, dies.

1963—Becomes a citizen of Ghana in Africa; dies on August 27.

CHAPTER NOTES

Chapter 1. Voice of Inspiration

1. William E. B. Du Bois, *The Autobiography of W.E.B. Du Bois: A Soliloquy on Viewing My Life from the Last Decade of Its First Century* (New York: International Publishers, 1968), pp. 255–259.

2. William E. B. Du Bois, letter to William English Walling, June 13, 1910, cited in Herbert Aptheker, ed., *The Correspondence of W.E.B. Du Bois* (Amherst: University of Massachusetts Press, 1973), pp. 170–171.

3. Du Bois, *Autobiography*, p. 259.

4. David Levering Lewis, *W.E.B. Du Bois: Biography of a Race* (New York: Henry Holt and Company, 1993), p. 409.

5. *The Crisis*, November 1910, cited in Nathan Huggins, ed., *W.E.B. Du Bois, Writings* (New York: Literary Classics of the United States, 1986), p. 1131.

6. Ibid., p. 1132.

7. Lewis, p. 413.

Chapter 2. Bright Youngster

1. Nathan Huggins, ed., *W.E.B. Du Bois: Writings* (New York: Literary Classics of the United States, 1986), p. 1281.

2. Manning Marable, *W.E.B. Du Bois: Black Radical Democrat* (Boston: Twayne Publishers, 1986), p. 3.

3. William E.B. Du Bois, *The Autobiography of W.E.B. Du Bois: A Soliloquy on Viewing My Life from the Last Decade of Its First Century* (New York: International Publishers, 1968), pp. 74–75.

4. David Levering Lewis, *W.E.B. Du Bois: Biography of a Race* (New York: Henry Holt and Company, 1993), p. 29.

5. Ibid., p. 32.

6. Du Bois, *Autobiography*, p. 79.

7. Ibid., p. 95.

8. Ibid., pp. 98–99.

9. Ibid., p. 99.

10. Herbert Aptheker, ed., *The Correspondence of W.E.B. Du Bois* (Amherst: University of Massachusetts Press, 1973), vol. 1, p. 5.

Chapter 3. College Whiz

1. Dan S. Green and Edwin Driver, eds., *W.E.B. Du Bois on Sociology and the Black Community* (Chicago: University of Chicago Press, 1978), p. 9.

2. Manning Marable, *W.E.B. Du Bois: Black Radical Democrat* (Boston: Twayne Publishers, 1986), p. 9.

3. David Levering Lewis, *W.E.B. Du Bois: Biography of a Race* (New York: Henry Holt and Company, 1993), pp. 60–61.

4. William E.B. Du Bois, letter to the Reverend Mr. Scudder, in *The Correspondence of W.E.B. Du Bois* (Amherst, Mass.: University of Massachusetts Press, 1973), p. 5.

5. William E. B. Du Bois, *The Autobiography of W.E.B. Du Bois: A Soliloquy on Viewing My Life from the Last Decade of Its First Century* (New York: International Publishers, 1968), pp. 114–118.

6. Ibid., pp. 128–129.

7. Green and Driver, p. 7.

8. Du Bois, *Autobiography*, p. 149.

9. Ibid., pp. 134–135.

10. Ibid., p. 146.

11. Lewis, pp. 101–102.

12. Ibid., p. 114.

13. Du Bois, *Autobiography*, pp. 170–171.

Chapter 4. Scholar and Professor

1. William E. B. Du Bois, *The Autobiography of W.E.B. Du Bois: A Soliloquy on Viewing My Life from the Last Decade of Its*

First Century (New York: International Publishers, 1968), p. 185.

2. David Levering Lewis, *W.E.B. Du Bois: Biography of a Race* (New York: Henry Holt and Company, 1993), pp. 152–154.

3. Tony Monteiro, "W.E.B. Du Bois: Scholar, Scientist, and Activist," *The W.E.B. Du Bois Virtual Library*, August 1997, <http://members.tripod.com/~DuBois/mont.html> (January 23, 1999).

4. Du Bois, p. 194.

5. Walter Goodman, "Pioneer in Sociology, Persevering Fighter for Civil Rights," *The New York Times*, February 7, 1997, p. B17.

6. Dan S. Green and Edwin Driver, eds., *W.E.B. Du Bois on Sociology and the Black Community* (Chicago: University of Chicago Press, 1978), pp. 6–8.

7. Ibid., pp. 10–16.

8. Lewis, p. 262.

9. Du Bois, p. 222.

10. Lewis, pp. 226–228.

11. Harold R. Isaacs, "Pan-Africanism as Romantic Racism," in Rayford W. Logan, ed., *W.E.B. Du Bois, A Profile* (New York: Hill and Wang, 1971), p. 228.

12. Lewis, pp. 251–252.

Chapter 5. Social Activist

1. William E. B. Du Bois, *The Autobiography of W.E.B. Du Bois: A Soliloquy on Viewing My Life from the Last Decade of Its First Century* (New York: International Publishers, 1968), pp. 242–244.

2. Manning Marable, *W.E.B. Du Bois: Black Radical Democrat* (Boston: Twayne Publishers, 1986), p. 50.

3. Louis R. Harlan, "Booker T. Washington and the Politics of Accommodation," in John Hope Franklin and August Meir, eds., *Black Leaders of the Twentieth Century* (Urbana: University of Illinois Press, 1982), pp. 2–5.

4. Du Bois, *Autobiography*, pp. 236–244.

5. Ibid., p. 237.

6. Ibid., p. 238.

7. W. E. B. Du Bois, *The Souls of Black Folk* (Chicago: A. C. McClurg and Company, 1903), p. 58.

8. W. E. B. Du Bois, in Herbert Aptheker, ed., *Writings by W.E.B. Du Bois in Periodicals Edited by Others* (New York: Kraus-Thomson, 1982), pp. 229–230.

9. David Levering Lewis, *W.E.B. Du Bois: Biography of a Race* (New York: Henry Holt and Company, 1993), pp. 322–323.

10. Du Bois, *Autobiography*, pp. 249–251.

11. Lewis, pp. 334–335.

12. Ibid., p. 342.

13. Ibid., p. 388.

14. Dan S. Green and Edwin D. Driver, eds., *W.E.B. Du Bois on Sociology and the Black Community* (Chicago: University of Chicago Press, 1978), p. 20.

15. Eric J. Sundquist, "W.E.B. Du Bois: Up to Slavery," *Commentary*, December 1986, p. 64.

16. Lewis, p. 439.

Chapter 6. Editor and Spokesman

1. William E.B. Du Bois, *The Autobiography of W.E.B. Du Bois: A Soliloquy on Viewing My Life from the Last Decade of Its First Century* (New York: International Publishers, 1968), pp. 258–262.

2. Richard Kostelanetz, *Politics in the African-American Novel: James Weldon Johnson, W.E.B. Du Bois, Richard Wright, and Ralph Ellison* (New York: Greenwood Press, 1991), p. 28.

3. David Levering Lewis, *W.E.B. Du Bois: Biography of a Race* (New York: Henry Holt and Company, 1993), p. 476.

4. Ibid., pp. 459–460.

5. Ibid., pp. 508–509.

6. W. E. B. Du Bois, *Dusk of Dawn*, p. 245, cited in Lewis, p. 521.

7. Lewis, p. 539.

8. Mark Ellis, "'Closing Ranks' and 'Seeking Honors': W.E.B. Du Bois in World War I," *The Journal of American History*, June 1992, pp. 96–99.

9. Manning Marable, *W.E.B. Du Bois: Black Radical Democrat* (Boston: Twayne Publishers, 1986), pp. 102–103.

Chapter 7. Civil Rights Leader

1. Elliott Rudwick, "W.E.B. Du Bois: Protagonist of the Afro-American Protest," in John Hope Franklin and August Meier, eds., *Black Leaders of the Twentieth Century* (Urbana: University of Illinois Press, 1982), p. 78.

2. Eric J. Sundquist, "W.E.B. Du Bois: Up to Slavery," *Commentary*, December 1986, p. 65.

3. David Levering Lewis, *W.E.B Du Bois: Biography of a Race* (New York: Henry Holt and Company, 1993), pp. 574–577.

4. Max Stanford, "The Pan African Party," *The Black Scholar*, February 1971, pp. 26–28.

5. Manning Marable, *W.E.B. Du Bois: Black Radical Democrat* (Boston: Twayne Publishers, 1986), pp. 118–120.

6. Sundquist, p. 66.

7. Ibid.

8. Marable, p. 135.

9. Ibid., p. 136.

10. William E. B. Du Bois, *The Autobiography of W.E.B. Du Bois: A Soliloquy on Viewing My Life from the Last Decade of Its First Century* (New York: International Publishers, 1968), pp. 289–290.

11. Andrew G. Paschal, ed., *A W.E.B. Du Bois Reader* (New York: The Macmillan Company, 1971), p. 376.

12. Rudwick, pp. 80–81.

13. Ibid., p. 82.

14. Marable, p. 144.
15. Du Bois, p. 308.
16. Herbert Aptheker, ed., *The Correspondence of W.E.B. Du Bois* (Amherst: University of Massachusetts Press, 1973), vol. 1, p. 1299.
17. Du Bois, p. 323.
18. Marable, pp. 162–163.
19. Ibid.
20. Ibid., pp. 164–165.
21. Ibid., p. 174.
22. Ibid., p. 174–175.
23. Ibid., pp. 175–176.

Chapter 8. Man of Controversy

1. Dan S. Green and Edwin D. Driver, eds., *W.E.B. Du Bois on Sociology and the Black Community* (Chicago: University of Chicago Press, 1978), p. 27.
2. Ibid., pp. 26–27.
3. Manning Marable, *W.E.B. Du Bois: Black Radical Democrat* (Boston: Twayne Publishers, 1986), p. 180.
4. Ibid.
5. Ibid., p. 181.
6. William E.B. Du Bois, *The Autobiography of W.E.B. Du Bois: A Soliloquy on Viewing My Life from the Last Decade of Its First Century* (New York: International Publishers, 1968), p. 379.
7. Ibid., p. 367.
8. Ibid., p. 379.
9. Green and Driver, p. 28.
10. Du Bois, pp. 394–395.
11. Ibid., p. 395.

Chapter 9. Expatriate

1. Manning Marable, *W.E.B. Du Bois: Black Radical Democrat* (Boston: Twayne Publishers, 1986), p. 203.

2. Ibid., p. 200.

3. Shirley Graham Du Bois, *His Day Is Marching On: A Memoir of W.E.B. Du Bois* (Philadelphia: J. B. Lippincott, 1971), p. 223.

4. Ibid.

5. Marable, pp. 192–193.

6. Richard Kostelanetz, *Politics in the African-American Novel* (New York: Greenwood Press, 1991), pp. 37–38.

7. Du Bois, pp. 235–238.

8. Ibid., p. 238.

9. Marable, p. 208.

10. Ibid., pp. 208–209.

11. Ibid.

12. Du Bois, pp. 316–317.

13. Ibid., p. 319–320.

14. Herbert Aptheker, "On Du Bois's Move to Africa," *Monthly Review*, December 1993, pp. 37–39.

15. Elliott Rudwick, "W.E.B. Du Bois: Protagonist of the Afro-American Protest," in John Hope Franklin and August Meier, eds., *Black Leaders of the Twentieth Century* (Urbana: University of Illinois Press, 1982), p. 83.

16. Du Bois, pp. 367–368.

17. "Honoring Dr. Du Bois," *Freedomways*, Spring 1968, p. 104.

18. Ibid., p. 108.

Chapter 10. Influential Thinker

1. Walter Goodman, "Pioneer in Sociology, Persevering Fighter for Civil Rights," *The New York Times*, February 7, 1997, p. B17.

2. Manning Marable, *W.E.B. Du Bois: Black Radical Democrat* (Boston: Twayne Publishers, 1986), p. viii.

3. David Levering Lewis, *W.E.B. Du Bois: Biography of a Race* (New York: Henry Holt and Company, 1993), p. 3.

4. Herbert Aptheker, "W.E.B. Du Bois: Struggle Not Despair," *Clinical Sociology Review*, 1990, pp. 58–68.

5. William E.B. Du Bois, *The Autobiography of W.E.B. Du Bois: A Soliloquy on Viewing My Life from the Last Decade of Its First Century* (New York: International Publishers, 1968), pp. 5–6.

6. Ibid.

7. W.E.B. Du Bois, "Advice to a Great-Grandson," *National Guardian*, March 5, 1956, cited in Philip S. Foner, ed., *W.E.B. Du Bois Speaks: Speeches and Addresses, 1920–1963* (New York: Pathfinder, 1991), pp. 292–293.

FURTHER READING

California Newsreel. *W.E.B. Du Bois: A Biography in Four Voices* (videocassette), 1995.

Cavan, Seamus. *W.E.B. Du Bois and Racial Relations.* Brookfield, Conn.: Millbrook Press, 1994.

Dornfield, Margaret. *W.E.B. Du Bois: Civil Rights.* Broomall, Pa.: Chelsea House, 1995.

Du Bois, Shirley Graham. *His Day is Marching On: A Memoir of W.E.B. Du Bois.* Philadelphia: Lippincott, 1971.

Du Bois, W.E.B. *The Autobiography of W.E.B. Du Bois: A Soliloquy on Viewing My Life from the Last Decade of its First Century.* New York: International Publishers, 1968.

———. *Dark Princess: A Romance.* Jackson, Miss.: University Press of Mississippi, 1995.

———. *Dusk of Dawn: An Essay Toward an Autobiography of a Race Concept.* New York: Harcourt-Brace, 1940.

———. *The Souls of Black Folk.* New York: Signet, 1995.

Foner, Philip S., ed. *W.E.B. Du Bois Speaks: Speeches and Addresses, 1890–1919.* New York: Pathfinder, 1988.

Hamilton, Virginia. *W.E.B. Du Bois: A Biography.* New York: Thomas Crowell, 1972.

Huggins, Nathan, ed. *W.E.B. Du Bois, Writings.* New York: The Library of America, 1986.

Stafford, Mark. *W.E.B. Du Bois: Scholar and Activist.* Broomall, Pa.: Chelsea House, 1990.

Sundquist, Eric J., ed. *The Oxford W.E.B. Du Bois Reader.* New York: Oxford University Press, 1996.

Tuttle, William Jr., ed. *W.E.B. Du Bois.* Englewood Cliffs, N.J.: Prentice-Hall, 1973.

Weinberg, Meyer, ed. *The World of W.E.B. Du Bois: A Quotation Sourcebook.* Westport, Conn.: Greenwood Press, 1992.

INTERNET ADDRESSES

The W.E.B. Du Bois Virtual University
<http://members.tripod.com/~DuBois/index.htm>

Voices Which Shaped Our Times: Marcus Garvey and W.E.B. Du Bois
<http://www.msu.edu/course/mc/112/1920s/ Garvey-DuBois/index.html>

Biographical Sketch of W.E.B. Du Bois
<http://www.dubois/c.org/html/DuBoisBio.html>

INDEX